CW00530366

For my family

First published 2001 by Uplands Books
1 The Uplands, Maze Hill, St Leonards-on-Sea
East Sussex TN38 0HL, England
www.pruetheobalds.com

ISBN 1 897951 38 8

Produced for Uplands Books by
The Foundry Creative Media Company Ltd,
Crabtree Hall, Crabtree Lane, Fulham, London SW6 6TY.

Printed in Barcelona, Spain by Sagrafic, S. L.

In the Company of BEARS

A Celebration for the Centenary of the Teddy Bear

by PRUE THEOBALDS

UPLANDS BOOKS

Contents

BEARS

A Celebration for the Centenary of the Teddy Bear

The Bears and I

My first significant encounter with bears was in 1983. For years I had been interested in early toys, and childhood memorabilia in general. My main interest, though, was dolls. I liked the miniature fashions and enjoyed drawing the different textured materials and the detailed lace and trimmings. Teddy bears to me then were just part of the general toy scene.

On that memorable day, nearly twenty years ago, I had gone to the Bethnal Green Museum of Childhood sketch-book in hand, intending to draw dolls, but it was there I met my destiny in the form of the Bethnal Green Museum collection of teddy bears.

It was with the Cattley Toys that I had my first eyeball to boot-button contact. This group of little bears with their period

clothes and childish possessions, including a miniature photograph album, radiated such a feeling of nostalgia that I found them irresistible. They brought back distant memories of my own long-forgotten years in the nursery, when I made clothes and accessories for my own childhood toys and, yes, I still have a minute photograph album too.

I think I realised then that teddy bears were potentially a much more interesting subject than dolls, whose porcelain faces don't age so endearingly as those of well loved bears. There was still the attraction of the period clothes to draw, but the outfits were more varied, and reflected historical events and social changes in a way that dolls' clothes don't. There was also the added allure of trying to capture the individual character of each bear.

There is something about a teddy bear, more than any other toy, that improves with age. The worn fur, the sagging limbs, the patched, mended and replaced parts all add to the charm and are what make each bear such a singular individual. One of the nicest things about bears is that the children who owned them speak to us through those boot-button, glass or even plastic eyes, the children who loved them and dressed them and made them the characters that they are.

I soon discovered that many of my elderly friends had treasured furry childhood companions tucked away. In Britain in the early eighties teddy bears were not so proudly displayed as they are now; there was still a certain amount of embarrassment about an adult clinging to a childhood toy. When word got round, however, that I liked drawing teddy bears I soon had a queue of venerable bears waiting patiently in my studio for their turn to be drawn.

In those days I was buying bears and other old toys in flea markets and junk shops. I would find bears, draw them, tidy them up and sell them, then buy some more.

I soon discovered, though, that the prices were climbing. I began to regret the bears I had sold, and decided to keep the ones I still had. I kept all the drawings, though, and as the bear supply in the junk shops dried up, or rather became too expensive, I took my sketch-book to the toy museums and found an endless source of wonderful characters to add to the collection in my bulging portfolio. Luckily I did not have to own bears in order to draw them.

This book contains the best of the many drawings of bears that I have done over the years, grouped into the decades in which they belong – from the early years of the twentieth century to the present day – a celebration of 100 years of wonderful teddy bears.

The First Teddy Bear – A Short History

In November 1902 Theodore Roosevelt paid a visit to Smedes, Mississippi to arbitrate on a border dispute. As he was a renowned hunter, a series of bear hunts were organised as entertainment while he was there, but after several days Roosevelt had not shot a single bear. Hoping to appease him, and to gain some good publicity photographs, his aides found a small bear cub, tied it to a tree, and confronted him with the perfect target. Roosevelt, however, refused to shoot the cub, not necessarily for sentimental reasons but probably more to save his macho image. A few days later a cartoon, drawn by Clifford Berryman, appeared in **The Washington Post** showing the President refusing to shoot the bear cub. It was captioned, "Drawing the line in Mississippi," referring to both the border dispute and the bear cub. The cartoon was amazingly popular and Clifford Berryman continued to draw the little bear on many other occasions.

It is said that a Brooklyn shopkeeper, Morris Michtom, placed the cartoon in his shop window beside a little toy bear that his wife had made. The toy sold immediately, and such was the demand for more that Morris Michtom eventually set up his own toy company in 1903, naming it The Ideal Toy and Novelty Company. Morris Michtom's son, Benjamin, claimed that his father had written to President Roosevelt for permission to call the bears "Teddy's Bears" and that the permission was granted; there is, however, no written evidence to support the claim.

Meanwhile in Germany, in the little southern town of Giengen-am-Brenz, a disabled seamstress called Margarete Steiff was gaining a reputation as a soft-toy maker. She began selling little felt animals in 1880 which proved immensely popular, and soon her toy business began to expand. Her nephew, Richard, who had studied sculpture in Stuttgart, joined his aunt's business in 1897 and by the end of October 1902 had designed the first toy bear using soft fur plush and pioneering movable joints. At first this bear was not very successful but at the 1903 Leipzig Spring Toy Fair it was spotted by an American buyer who immediately placed an order for three thousand and the rest, as they say, is history.

In Britain many early bears were known as Edward. Perhaps, as the name Theodore is not so common in Britain, many people thought that Teddy was an abbreviation of Edward and they associated the name with King Edward VII.

Edouard, 1905 Steiff

Chapter One

1902-1910

The Cattley Toys

The Cattley Toys at the Bethnal Green Museum are a group of nine little bears, some rabbits and an amazing elephant called Pumpie.

They belonged to the Cattley children, Maud, Donald, Constance, Nellie and Gilbert who were born between 1885 and 1892.

The bears are all dressed in wonderful turn-of-the-century clothes made by the children themselves with some help from Edith, their mother. As well as numerous outfits, including full sets of underwear, the toys have a miniature photograph album displaying tiny sepia photographs taken in various settings, including a seaside group posed on the beach during a summer holiday. There is also an album of small watercolour paintings, again portraits of the toys wearing outfits selected from their extensive wardrobes.

Teddy Girl

Teddy Girl became the most famous bear in the world when she was sold in 1994 to Mr Sekiguchi of the Sun Arrow Toy Company for the record auction price of £110,000. She now resides in the Izu Teddy Bear Museum in Japan. In 1988 in my anthology **The Teddy Bear** I unwittingly wrote a prophetic caption to my drawing of Teddy Girl stating, "*Early bears such as this are much sought after and fetch record prices at auction*"!

I drew Teddy Girl on a trip to Edinburgh in 1987. On arrival at Colonel Bob Henderson's house on a cold afternoon in late November, I was ushered into the front room. There was Teddy Girl sitting waiting for me on a table in the middle of the room, looking very small and vulnerable.

As I sat down to draw, Colonel Henderson and his housekeeper both drew up chairs and sat down facing me. Neither of them spoke but sat rigidly, with their eyes fixed on me. Once, Colonel Henderson seemed about to speak but he was sharply rapped on the knuckles. I felt tense and self-conscious, and wondered how I could draw with them both staring at me. But also looking at me was Teddy Girl, with that wonderful expression of hers. I concentrated hard and managed to focus on the bear and the job in hand, and pretended there was no one else in the room.

I eventually got enough information down in my sketchbook to enable me to do a final drawing once I was back in the more relaxed atmosphere of my own studio.

As soon as I announced that I had finished, Colonel Henderson sprang to life. Tea was brought in and I was regaled with the fruits of his years of research into the philosophy surrounding the bear. He spoke about Russia, folklore, American Indians, the bear as an icon of love and care, and the work of Good Bears of the World, of which he was co-founder. I learnt that Teddy Girl had started life as Teddy Boy and had belonged originally to his older brother who had magnanimously passed the bear on to him. Later, Colonel Bob's daughter Cynthia inherited him and changed the name to Teddy Girl. Teddy Girl it has most famously remained.

After tea I was taken on a grand tour of the house. Each room seemed to contain more bears than the previous one. Even the bathroom had bear-shaped bottles filling every shelf. In the study I was amazed to see a desk piled high, and I mean high, with unopened letters. I imagined that somewhere in their midst were the two I had sent in an attempt to arrange the current meeting. No wonder I had received no reply and had resorted to the telephone! Colonel Bob dismissed the pile of letters with a wave of the hand, saying he could no longer cope with mail. His housekeeper, who could only walk with the aid of a Zimmer frame, was unable to come upstairs. Obviously secretarial duties were not in her remit.

When I finally got the last bus back into central Edinburgh my mind was buzzing with bear awareness, or in Colonel Bob's words, "Teddy Bear Consciousness". I began to realise then that the teddy bear was far more than just a child's toy.

Good Bears of the World was founded in 1973 in Berne, Switzerland, by Jim Ownby, an American broadcaster and journalist, and Colonel Bob Henderson. It aimed to "Promote humanitarian treatment and benefaction for the young around the world." The idea was to present Good Bear teddies to sick or distressed children and the young at heart, either in hospital or at home. The organisation was founded on October 27th, President Theodore Roosevelt's birthday, and this day was nominated Good Bear Day in his honour. Good Bears of the World is still a very active organisation and must have given consolation to countless unhappy people during the years it has been in existence.

Alfonzo

lfonzo is a truly wonderful bear with an amazing and well-documented proven history. He is a red Steiff bear bought in 1908 by the Grand Duke of Russia as a present for his daughter, Princess Xenia Georgievna. The Princess's governess made him a little Cossack suit in which to accompany his young owner on a visit to Buckingham Palace in 1914. This visit coincided with the outbreak of the First World War and it was decided that Princess Xenia should remain in Britain. In 1919 the Princess's father was killed during the Russian Revolution; consequently Alfonzo and his young owner never returned to Russia.

I remember my first encounter with the shop Teddy Bears of Witney. It was October 1984 and my husband and I were driving through the Cotswolds in the early hours of a Sunday morning. We made a detour to Witney to see if we could locate an antique shop selling old teddy bears that I had recently read about. Sure enough in the High Street was a tiny antique shop. We both squinted through the window to see if we could spot any old teddy bears.

Anyone visiting the shop today would find it much expanded and selling a magnificent selection of bears old and new. They would also be able to meet many famous teddy characters in the rapidly expanding museum section.

The Princess married an American in 1921 and Alfonzo moved with her to the United States, remaining with her until her death in 1965. In 1989, the Princess's daughter sent him to Christie's, in London, to be sold at auction. He was bought by Ian Pout, owner of the wonderful shop Teddy Bears of Witney, where he now has pride of place. Ian arranged for Steiff to make a limited edition Alfonzo which was so successful that it was followed by a "baby Alfonzo" edition.

Ian kindly invited me to do a portrait of Alfonzo shortly after he had bought him.

He was a delightful little bear to draw and has a particularly appealing expression. In spite of his royal connections he does not look at all snooty, as do many of the early Steiff bears. He has the sort of expression that seems to say he would tell you his amazing history if he could just get his mind together, but he is only little and it was all so long ago.

Rudolph

Rudolph was one of the first bears I drew from John and Judy Sparrow's lovely collection at the Bear Museum in Petersfield. He is an early Steiff bear that had recently been acquired in a somewhat frail condition. When Judy repaired him she discovered airgun pellets in his voice box but, thanks to her careful surgery and his nice Edwardian dress (as would have been worn by a little boy of the period), he is now fit to be seen and admired by all.

Aloysius

Aloysius is an early American bear, made in 1907 by Morris Michtom's Ideal Toy and Novelty Company. He spent fifty years languishing on a shelf in Ladd's dry goods store and delicatessen in Maine. After the owner had seen the actor Peter Bull on television, promoting his new book **Bear With Me,** she sent him the bear to add to his collection. Peter Bull immediately christened him Delicatessen after the shop where he had spent so many dreary years. But Delicatessen's life was destined to change dramatically. In 1977 Granada Television bought the film rights to Evelyn Waugh's **Brideshead Revisited**. When filming began, a few years later, a suitable teddy bear was required to play the part of Aloysius, Sebastian Flyte's teddy. Peter Bull, with his stage connections and teddy bear collection, was an obvious source of recruitment and Delicatessen landed the part. Once the epic television serialisation of the book had been shown around the world, the bear became so famous that his name was changed, by deed poll, to Aloysius.

The House of Nisbet made the first replica of Aloysius, under his original name, Delicatessen. While the bear was temporarily resident with them in Somerset, Jack Wilson gave me permission to do a portrait of him. I made a trip down to Somerset, eagerly clutching sketch-book and pencils, only to find Aloysius was being exhibited in London. By the time I returned home Aloysius was back in Somerset. I eventually tracked him down, though, and was finally able to do my portrait.

Aloysius is a much-travelled bear. After Peter Bull's death he resided for a while at the Teddy Bear Museum in Stratford-upon-Avon, then returned to the United States to join the Volpps' famous collection in California. After a while he obviously got itchy paws and a touch of homesickness as he is now back in Britain, reunited with his soul mate, Peter Bull's miniature bear, Theodore. They are now both on permanent show with Ian Pout's other famous bears at Teddy Bears of Witney.

Peter Bull's book **Bear With Me** *was published in 1969. In this book he declared himself a bear lover, or arctophile, a name which I believe he invented. This was the start of what was perceived as respectability for bear collectors. In 1984 I was promised an introduction to Peter Bull by a mutual acquaintance, but sadly he died before I was able to meet him. It was really Peter Bull and his books which started the British bear collecting mania.*

Mascot Bear

Mascot Bear lives in the Edinburgh Museum of Childhood where I drew him in 1986. He wears the uniform of the Edinburgh Company Royal Army Medical Corps Volunteers. The 2nd Division Volunteer Medical Staff was raised in 1886 and was later amalgamated with the Royal Army Medical Corps in 1908, which is probably the year that the bear dates from.

Jester

Jester is a very interesting bear. He was discovered in a remote cottage in Scotland in 1991 and was sent to Christie's for auction the same year. As an early, white clown bear, 70cm tall and in superb condition, he was one of the highlights of the sale but because of his unknown origins the bidding was tentative. He was bought by a Dutch collector who instigated further research in Britain and America, but to no avail.

Jester was later returned to Christie's for their winter sale in December 1995 and was purchased by Jürgen and Marianne Cieslik, publishers of the German teddy bear collector's magazine, **Teddybär und seine Freunde**. Jürgen and Marianne, having spent much time researching the numerous German teddy bear manufacturers and studying endless archive catalogues, had discovered Jester's true origins. He had been made by the Nuremberg based toy factory of Wilhelm Strunz in 1909, as was proved by photographs and descriptions of clown bears in various sizes shown in the Strunz catalogue for that year. Jester is now exhibited annually during the last weekend in April at the great Teddybär Total fair in Hennef, near Bonn.

The Strunz cloth and felt toy factory had been founded in 1902 and was a permanent

thorn in the side of Steiff, with whom they had many a legal dispute.

When I first became interested in old toys I would often frequent the street markets in Brighton and was familiar with the various antique and junk shops that were likely sources of childhood memorabilia. Once old teddy bears became the focus of my interest, I soon discovered Sue Pearson's recently opened little shop in the Lanes at 13 ½ Prince Albert Street. Sue has spent most of her life involved in antiques and is very knowledgeable about old toys as well as bears. She is very generous with her knowledge and has always been happy to give me her opinion on various bears and other oddities that I have shown her over the years. Her tiny shop is a magical world and a magnet for bear lovers worldwide.

Valentina

Valentina is also an early Strunz bear belonging to Sue Pearson. She wears a lovely grey silk dress trimmed with antique lace, made by the mother of the original owner from one of her own dresses. The bear was a St Valentine's Day present from Sue's husband, hence the name.

Little Tommy Tittlemouse

Little Tommy Tittlemouse is another old bear from the Bethnal Green Collection. He dates from the early years of the century and up until a few years ago received a birthday card each year from "father". When I drew him in 1983 he was seventy-four, although his alert little beady eyes and cheerful expression defy his total baldness and obvious age.

Bruin and Teddy

ruin and Teddy are also to be found in the Edinburgh Museum of Childhood. They were bought in Leeds Market in 1909 for two little sisters. They were obviously well cared for by their young owners, who dressed them in these nice warm clothes to help them combat the severities of a Scottish winter.

The combination of the names Bruin and Teddy is an interesting one, as for the first three years of its existence the teddy bear was as yet unnamed and was often referred to as bruin. There is no record of the name Teddy being used prior to 1906.

The bear mania that hit America during the early years of the twentieth century was obviously fuelled by events in the White House. By 1906 bears (or bruins as they were often called) were seen, by some, as political propaganda and members of the opposition party were at first reluctant to buy what they perceived as a Republican mascot for their children.
Playthings, *a contemporaneous toy trade magazine, had no such qualms. "Young America had christened them," it confidently asserts in 1906, "appropriately too. Isn't the President the hero of every boy who longs to grow big enough to hold a gun to shoot bears and some day do just the very same things that "Teddy" Roosevelt does? So Teddy the bears were named and as Teddy they are known now the length and breadth of our country, as well as on the other side of the Atlantic."*

Early English teddy riding a German pull-along bear

Chapter Two

1910–1920

Albert

Albert is another lovely Steiff bear from the Petersfield collection, dating from about 1910. He was rescued in an extremely frail condition, but Judy Sparrow, being a very skilled needlewoman, managed to repair him. He has now gained an added history since I drew him back in the early eighties. In 1993 he was stolen from the museum, together with many other of the Sparrows' valuable collection, and was missing for four years until one of his admirers spotted him in an antique shop. Although he had been altered to change his appearance, he was recognised and restored to his rightful place. Judy Sparrow had, in the meantime, made a most amazing replica of him using an old blanket which came closest to recreating his completely bald look. She said she found making the replica a very therapeutic exercise. Judy also wrote a touching little book about the theft of her bears called **Bears in the Rainbow**, in which she weaves a healing magic over the memory of her lost treasures.

Tim

Tim is another bear from Sue Pearson's personal collection. He is a very small, apricot-coloured, early Farnell, dating from about 1911. He wears his original clothes, consisting of a purple serge suit with a sailor collar and a matching hat, which he wears nonchalantly slung across his back on a piece of elastic. As I was about to draw him, Sue thought he needed some luggage. So she

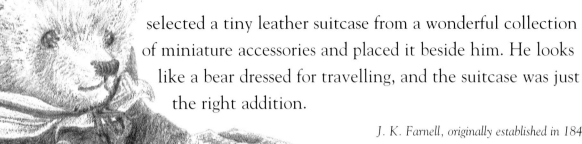

selected a tiny leather suitcase from a wonderful collection of miniature accessories and placed it beside him. He looks like a bear dressed for travelling, and the suitcase was just the right addition.

J. K. Farnell, originally established in 1840, began to produce soft toys in 1897 and were probably the first British toy factory to make teddy bears. The earliest Farnell bears appear to date from around 1908. In 1921 they opened a new factory which they called The Alpha Works, the teddy bears from this period were known as Alpha bears and the Alpha trade mark was registered in 1925. Farnell were one of the most respected of all the British teddy bear manufacturers. They opened a factory in my own home town of Hastings in 1959 but, sadly, as teddy bear sales declined during the sixties, so did the fortunes of Farnell. They were bought by a finance company in 1968 and the factory eventually closed in 1970.

Teddy

Teddy was one of the first bears I drew that still belonged to its original owner. He was given to her in 1911 when her younger sister was born and he has remained with her ever since, presiding in a lugubrious fashion over all the family comings and goings. He is completely bald, has undergone some painful surgery on his ears and suffers from foot problems but, none the less, he is a much loved and very desirable "centre seam" Steiff.

The centre seam down the faces of some old Steiff bears came about because pieces for only six bears could be cut from one length of fabric, but a seventh bear could be squeezed out if the face was cut in two sections. As these bears are six times rarer than the others they are always much sought-after and can command higher prices. They would, of course, have to be in a far better condition than poor old Teddy.

Gilmour

Gilmour was bought in Ireland but is possibly of English make. He was given to his owner, Margaret, for Christmas 1911 and accompanied her to Celbridge Collegiate Girls' School and later to Trinity College, Dublin. He remained with her all her life, even during her final years in a nursing home. I drew him in the Burrows collection in Bath.

The Titanic Bear

The Titanic Bear is only fifteen centimetres tall and was probably made by the German company Gebrüder Bing. It was given to Gaspare Gatti by his young son, Vittorio, before he took up the post of catering manager on the Titanic and sailed off on that fateful voyage. After the disaster Gatti's body was one of the many recovered by the cable ship, SS Minia. The little teddy was found in his pocket with his meerschaum pipe, both of which were returned to his widow.

The little bear was obviously destined to be a survivor as he was also recovered after the Gatti home was demolished by a bomb during the Second World War. For many years he lay in a drawer, wrapped in some of Mrs Gatti's underwear, until, in 1990, the family decided to give the bear and the meerschaum pipe to the Museum of Childhood in Ribchester in Lancashire.

The owners of the museum, Ankie and David Wilde, had some discussions with me about the possibility of publishing a small illustrated book relating the bear's life story but, unfortunately, I was too busy at the time. In 1992, however, the British toy maker, Merrythought, made a limited edition of the little teddy to mark the 80th anniversary of the sinking of the Titanic. He was displayed in a splendid box which included his baggage ticket and the story of the ill-fated voyage. In 1995 the Wildes retired, closed the museum and sold their collection, including the little Gatti bear.

In 1912 Steiff produced some black Titanic mourning bears specifically for the English market. These bears have a red felt backing to the eyes which seems to give them an even more mournful expression. When they come up for auction they are usually in mint condition as, owing to their sad associations, they were seldom played with.

Mark Anthony

Mark Anthony was one of my earlier finds. I had bought a couple of other bears and a little Chinese doll from a local junk shop for a few pounds and this bear was "thrown in" owing to his distressed state. He had only one arm and no ears but he did have a wonderful growl and rather surprising eyebrows. I unpicked the eyebrows and borrowed some ears from a tattered but obliging lion. This was why he became known as Mark Anthony. I never sold him because of his one arm and disintegrating feet. I am glad he is still with me as he is one of my earlier bears, I am not sure of his country of origin but he could be American or German.

Tubby Toes

Tubby Toes is one of our family bears and was a surprise find in the mid-seventies. My husband, having an interest in antique glass, successfully bid for a large mixed lot at our local auction house. Amongst the pieces of glass and miscellaneous junk that he brought home was a box bulging with old dolls' clothes which I was delighted to take off his hands. As I looked through the box I was surprised to find, buried amongst the dolls' clothes, a smaller box in which lay a tiny teddy bear with beady eyes. In the box with him was a little bookcase full of tiny school books, marked with his name, Tubby Toes. He was also accompanied by two tiny dolls made out of paper and ribbon, two little cardboard musical instruments, a minute painting on a matchstick easel and other small doll's house accessories. When I was researching early bear books for my anthology I came across a little book, published in 1913, called **Tim Tubby Toes**. I think our little bear is of a similar date and was probably named after the character in the book.

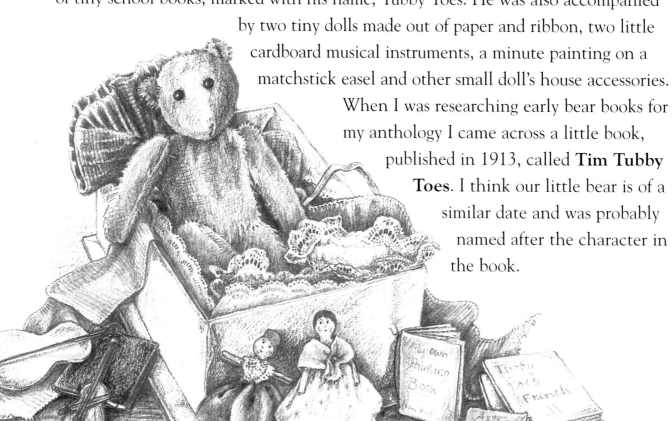

Digby

Digby is another miniature bear that belonged to a very dear friend, Anna Awdry. He has a wooden stick that runs through a hole in his paw and was presumably a mechanical bear of some kind, probably made by the German company Gebrüder Bing, although he has obviously long forgotten the purpose of the stick (or what it was attached to). This drawing reminds me of a very happy afternoon in 1989 when Tubby Toes, and a more recently acquired Sophie, enjoyed tea in Anna's garden under the apple blossom with Digby and the rest of her bears. It was a memorable meeting after years of only knowing each other through letters.

During the First World War German production of teddy bears was much reduced and all imports to Britain were halted. Most of the German factories turned their skills to producing equipment for the war effort and many members of staff were recruited into the army. There was, though, a growing demand for teddy bears in Britain and America and it was during this period that many new British soft toy manufacturers came on the scene, producing well made bears that were distinctly different from their German counterparts. I have recently been repairing a very nice British bear dating from about 1914. On removing his growler I found it bore a stamp which, although rather blurred, appears to read "manufactured by British labour".

Master Teddy

Master Teddy is a very early British character bear made in 1915 by the Chiltern Toy Works. I drew this delightfully cheeky little fellow on a recent visit to the Petersfield Bear Museum, having heard that Judy Sparrow had acquired him. Judy's bear is unusual because his chameleon-like eyes, capable of swivelling in all directions, are opaque white and blue glass, the more usual colour being opaque brown. In the museum he is displayed with this tiny Farnell mascot bear from the First World War wearing original, patriotically coloured, hand-knitted clothing and enthusiastically waving a Union Jack.

The Chiltern Toy Works were founded during the early years of the twentieth century by a German, Joseph Eisenmann. Together with his partner, Leon Rees, also a naturalised German and married to Eisenmann's daughter, they introduced some of the first British-made teddy bears. Joseph died in 1919 and Leon inherited the business. Together with Harry Stone, who had previously been with J.K.Farnell, they set up a business called H.G.Stone and Company to manufacture toys at the Chiltern Toy Works, using the Chiltern trade mark. In 1924 the name Chiltern Toys was registered as the company name.

Several British manufacturers, Farnell, William J. Terry and, later, Merrythought all gave their bears very distinctive webbed paws, as can be seen on this bear. William J. Terry were another of the first pioneering British toy manufacturers. They were established in 1890 and began making bears sometime around the First World War.

Sailor Bear

Sailor Bear, in his First World War uniform, is another of my very early encounters at the Bethnal Green Museum. When I first drew him it was assumed that because of his early date he must be German, but subsequent research suggests that he was more likely to have been made by one of the early British manufacturers, Farnell or William J. Terry.

The Colonel

The Colonel, another bear I decided not to sell, is German but of unknown make, dating from about 1914. I bought him, together with a little Steiff monkey (because they had always been together), at the time when prices first started to rise. I remember being shocked at paying £50 for them and decided, then, not to let any of my remaining bears go.

The Colonel, in his striped jumper bearing my grandfather's First World War miniature medals, and Theo, a thirties Farnell bear, became my most well-known bears. I drew them often and introduced them into several books. But, one sad day in 1994 the Colonel, Theo and Jacko, the monkey, got left on a London bus. They had been helping out at a trade fair at Earls Court. We were all tired and somehow when I got off the bus at Hammersmith the bears and Jacko went on to Chiswick. I haven't seen the Colonel or Jacko since, although Theo made a spectacular return and is still with me, a slightly chastened bear. You can read his story in a later chapter. Funnily enough, in my book **The Great Expedition** I portrayed the Colonel as an intrepid explorer who always managed to get lost. I never dreamt that he would fulfil this rôle so accurately in reality.

Sue Nicoll of the Romsey Bear Company made a limited edition replica of the Colonel after he had gone missing. Sue managed to portray a lot of his character even though she only had my drawings to go by. The replica had cardboard medals and a map of India to help him find his way around.

Brother Ted, English clown bear

Chapter Three

1920-1930

Buttons

The twenties were known as the dog years as there was a sudden decline in the popularity of the teddy bear because toy dogs, as well as real dogs, were now the new fashion accessory.

Buttons was made in about 1923 by the German manufacturers, Schuco, famous for their mechanical toys. He is known as a bell-hop yes-no bear and has a little tail which acts as a lever to make him nod or shake his head. He was always enjoyed by children when he accompanied me on a school visit, although he has now been retired from the school circuit as he was beginning to find the constant questioning a bit too much.

Originally, he would have had the most wonderful elongated feet, but sadly they have been worn away, possibly as a result of constant bell-hopping.

Pongo

Pongo was a bear that I found in a box of bits in a junk shop. He was filthy and smelt disgusting, hence his name. In my ignorance I plunged him into a basin of hot water and detergent and gave him a good bath. The difference was amazing. He emerged a completely different colour, but had to sit on the boiler for a week to get dry. I now know that you should never wash an old bear, however dirty or smelly. I also know now that he was a nice Chad Valley bear, dating from the twenties and was filled with the new kapok filling. He should have had a button bearing the "Aerolite" trade mark introduced by Chad Valley about this time, but I don't think he did, unless it went down the plug hole.

After drawing Pongo, I sold him to a bear repairer who used him as an advertisement for her bear hospital facilities. I would meet him at bear fairs, swathed in bandages, looking decidedly woebegone but resigned to the fact that he was a bear who was always destined to draw the short straw in life.

Josephine

Josephine is a Chiltern Hugmee bear made by the British company, H.G.Stone. Being a nice sized, reasonably slim bear she fits into a wide range of dolls' clothes and enjoyed dressing up in this stylish, contemporary outfit. She has posed for me frequently in many different clothes and situations.

In the years after the First World War German goods were not available in Britain. This enabled the newly fledged British companies to expand. Much of the mohair plush fabric used for teddy bear manufacturing was produced in Yorkshire and had been exported to Germany and America. Now there was an opportunity for Britain to make use of its own product.

The British bears of this period tend to have glass eyes, usually made of clear glass with painted backs. Squeakers replaced the growlers of the previous two decades and soft kapok was used for stuffing, instead of the harder wood-wool. Kapok was cheaper and more readily available in Britain as it was supplied by the British colonies. It had been pioneered as a filling for life belts during the First World War. British bears no longer copied the German models but were recognisable in their own right.

Pooh

This "Pooh" bear is English and was made in 1926. The bear is based on the A.A.Milne character, Winnie-the-Pooh who made his first appearance in 1926 and was immediately very popular. This little look-alike is in Pollock's Toy Museum, London. He wears hand-knitted clothing, suitable for a blustery day and came to the museum with his own chair, tin telephone and friends Kanga and Roo. I have drawn him here accompanied by a velvet piglet from my own collection.

The real Winnie-the-Pooh, on whom the stories were based, was an Alpha Farnell bear, bought in Harrods in 1921. When E.H.Shepard started working on the illustrations for the books he did not find the Farnell bear particularly inspiring, so he based his Pooh character on his son's bear, Growler, a 1906 Steiff. I tried to track down Growler in 1987 but discovered that he had emigrated to Canada and had had a terminal encounter with a dog.

Rupert

Rupert is another well-known, and still much loved teddy bear character. He first appeared in the newspaper **The Daily Express** in 1920 and was very popular from the start. Many teddy bears during this period acquired Rupert's typical checked trousers and scarf. This bear, wearing clothes knitted by the owner's mother, has the blue jumper and grey and white checked trousers in which Rupert made his first appearance. Later, when the illustrator Alfred Bestall took over from the originator, Mary Tourtel, the jumper was changed to the familiar red and the scarf and trousers to yellow.

Guinea-Pig Jack

Guinea-Pig Jack is called after a well-known Bath pedlar who died in 1907. He wears a little red coat of an earlier date, modelled on the one worn by the famous Bath character. I met this little Dean's Rag Book bear in the Burrow's Toy Museum in Bath in the early eighties. The museum has since closed.

Happy

Happy, a 1926 Steiff bear, was sold by Sothebys in 1989 for the then record price of £55,000. She was bought by the American collector, Paul Volpp, as an anniversary present for his wife Rosemary. Happy is made of rare "dual" coloured mohair and has very large eyes which give her a particularly endearing look.

I met Happy in Germany in 1996, while attending the enormous Teddybär Total fair in Hennef. We happened to be staying in the same hotel as Rosemary and Paul Volpp and one morning we shared a breakfast table with them. Rosemary takes Happy with her everywhere, so when I said I would love to meet her she immediately appeared from under the table, wrapped in a

soft baby blanket for protection. She peeped out at us with her large, soft eyes and I could see why she has that special appeal. When I asked Rosemary if I could include Happy in this book she said, "Sharing is one of a bear's most essential parts!" Happy has been fulfilling this rôle to full capacity since she came into Rosemary's life.

Piccolo

These little bears, only 6cm tall, were made in the mid-twenties by the German factory Schreyer und Co. under their trade name of Schuco. They were called Piccolo bears and were intended to be given away as free publicity. The early ones, like mine, have flat pieces of felt for hands and feet. These are attached to the ends of the internal structure which is all metal. My little bear wears a tiny Pickelhaube helmet which I found in a box of buttons bought many years ago at a jumble sale. I have drawn him peeping out of an inkwell box which is of a similar age; it provides a useful refuge for him in the hurly-burly of my studio.

Some of the larger bears in the Piccolo series contained powder compacts or small scent bottles and were made in a variety of colours. It is interesting to note that the teddy bear was still a cult symbol for young women right through the twenties.

Teddy

After sixty-one years of loving disinterest
Repaired yet retired to lurk in attics
In damp plastic boxes of last season's dresses
He returned to daylight more faded than ever
To win the school prize for the oldest bear.

The sepia photo of my two-year old mother
Beaming plumply by her brand new bear
Shows little resemblance to the patched bald figure
Who sits before me, staring cockeyed
With the two black buttons I sewed as a child;

An over-large nose, bright red and padded
To replace the hessian eaten by moths,
And tartan paws, themselves now faded,
But once the latest fashion in bears;

A lopsided patch in his lefthand side
Covers the wound of a vital operation
To save his life from a rusty squeaker
And fatten him up on a diet of stockings.

My constant companion in earlier days,
I cried all night in my hospital cot
When moved by a nurse who did not understand
My fear I would never see him again.

I'm not a hoarder but in eight house moves
He has gone with me, along with my wife
And successive children, journeying calmly
From loft to attic, biding his time,
Knowing his moment of glory would come

As it did, with an Easter Egg prize for Lucy
And a commendation for an ancient bear
Who will never grace an attic again.

Brian Hick

Teddy

Teddy was first introduced to me through the poem and I was delighted to meet him eventually, in the fur. Finding a poem inspired by an actual teddy bear was one of the triggers that started me thinking about the possibilities of compiling an anthology of teddy bears. A little while later when the publisher, Blackie, put the suggestion of an anthology to me I had already mapped out some of the potential contents and was keen to pursue the idea. I have drawn Teddy here wearing the remains of a jumper worn by Brian at the age of three. The scarf is a more recent present knitted by Brian's daughter, Lucy.

Peter Bear

Peter Bear is one of a group of very rare bears that came to light in the late seventies. Carol Ann Stanton, the well-known doll maker, told me the interesting story of her involvement in the arrival of these previously unknown rarities.

During the seventies, Carol had a shop in Camden Passage, in London, and also a stall in the Portobello Road Antique Market. One day an eighteen-year-old German, speaking practically no English, appeared at her stall and thrust a box into her hands. On opening the box she was amazed to find this unusual bear in mint condition, complete with a catalogue naming the factory where he had been made, the Gebrüder Süssenguth toy factory in Neustadt bei Coburg, Thuringia. The catalogue showed a range of "lifelike" bears in different colours, naming them "Peter Bears". Other pages in the catalogue showed the dolls that had been the main output of the factory. The young man asked Carol if she would buy the bear, which she readily agreed to do. He then announced that he could get some more.

Some weeks later, the same young man turned up again with sixty-five more bears, in a range of colours, all in their original boxes. Carol was completely taken aback but somehow managed to find the money to buy the complete stock.

The story eventually emerged that the bears had been found abandoned in the closed-down factory, where they had been made. Apparently these lifelike bears with their "googly" eyes, moving tongue and fearsome teeth had not been a huge success with the young when they were first introduced in 1925. The factory, which was in East Germany, had gone into decline and had eventually closed down, leaving the remaining stock behind. The young man who found the bears tried to sell them in Germany but at that time there was not much German interest in teddy bears. He did manage to sell the two largest bears from the collection to a couple of museums in West Germany and two years later he brought the rest to Britain.

Two Little Gustav Förster Bears

Carol later went on a trip to Germany, to the great traditional toy making area of Neustadt. She was taken to a primitive teddy bear factory where a group of women were making cheap teddy bears for sale at local fairs and carnivals. Carol, disappointed with the quality of the bears shown to her, produced from her pocket a miniature bear that she often took on her travels. She explained that she was looking for similarly well-made bears. The women looked surprised, and one of them left the room to return with an almost identical bear. Both bears had been made during the twenties by the same cottage industry and had been marketed by Gustav Förster.

French Bear by Pintel

Chapter Four

1930-1940

Queen

Queen was my original childhood bear. She started life in India in the mid-thirties and was called Andrew. My father was in the army and the early years of my life included a lot of travelling. Whenever we travelled, our toys were all squashed into a large kit bag. We came back to England and eventually settled in York, where the toys were gleefully unpacked. When Andrew emerged from the kit bag his nose was all squashed sideways and, I am ashamed to say, I rejected him. A golly I was given at about that time became my special toy. I dressed it in a frilly blue dress and called it the Queen of the Fairies.

It was the Queen of the Fairies that I clutched in the air-raid shelter during the war and that suffered my childhood illnesses with me. I can remember, one fearful night, burying my feverish face in its frilly dress when the night-light flared up and set fire to the **Doctor Dolittle** book on the near-by chest of drawers.

Poor Andrew was forgotten about until my younger brother gathered him up, together with my older sister's bear, and they became King and Queen of his nursery kingdom, where every toy had a position from Lord Chancellor to royal washerwoman. I became involved again and made elaborate wardrobes for them all. We collected miniatures and made little accessories for the toys to use. I still have a tiny photograph album and a napkin in a silver napkin ring, which had once been part of a propelling pencil. King survives with my brother's family, somewhat saggy and lacking in fur, but still retaining an authoritarian look. Queen, alas, was discovered years later when my mother was moving house. The poor old bear was found in a box at the back of a shed, with the royal washerwoman (a knitted penguin). Sadly, both toys were completely moth-ridden and beyond saving.

I found this Dean's bear recently. It is the right age and has very similar looks to how I remember Queen. King is a Dean's bear and I am sure both bears would have

been bought from the same source. I have drawn her wearing the kind of dress that
I can remember making for the royal wardrobe. She is also wearing a little brooch,
found when picnicking on the Yorkshire Moors, all those
years ago. I still have the brooch and, of
course, the photograph album.

King

King as he is now with his two remaining companions, Eli and Evans

King

He wasn't called King when we first met.
He belonged to my sister before me
But you could tell by the way his eyes were set
That he was not just any old pet
But a wise old bear – a really good bet
To put in charge of the nursery.

He wasn't the kind of bear to dress up
Or involve in let's pretend.
He was in charge, and when he was there
Everyone else was aware of the bear
With his steady gaze and unwinking stare
That would see things through to the end.

He wasn't sad but he did not smile.
He took things in his stride.
A serious far off look had he
He never said very much to me
(That's because he was thinking you see)
And he had Queen by his side.

There were others around to do the jobs
That needed to be done:
Prime Minister Jarvis to govern the land,
The Army had Eli to lead the band,
The Navy – Evans' steady hand
But they knew that King was the special one.

Simon Theobalds

Teddy Valena

Teddy Valena was my cousin's bear. She also started life in India, being bought at the Army and Navy Stores in Bombay in 1933. I have a photograph of a group of hot, irritable-looking children in muslin dresses and frilled shirts, taken at a party in Quetta. My cousin, my older sister and I, aged about ten months, are sitting in the front row and my cousin is clutching Teddy Valena. The curious thing is that although the teddy bear had, by then, only been around for about four years, she is already eyeless and looks fairly distressed.

Teddy Valena was inherited by the next sibling cousin in the family and is still with her, having led an adventurous and much-travelled life. About fifteen years ago she was in such a frail condition that my aunt asked a friend to repair her. The poor lady, when faced with such a disintegrating old bear, thought the only thing she could do was to enclose each part of her in a piece of nylon stocking. The finished result was very strange. When I drew her I had to try to see the bear through the nylon, like "looking through a glass darkly". But, the worst crime of all was that Teddy Valena was given eyes. My cousin was horrified. Teddy Valena had never had eyes, as long as anyone could remember, just blue crayon round the holes. Now, with eyes, she had lost the familiar myopic look – she was no longer Teddy Valena.

Theo

Theo is an English Farnell bear that I bought in the sale room in Battle, near Hastings. He was part of a large collection of toys and books that had come from the attic of a house owned by two elderly sisters. With him came a Dean's Betty Oxo doll and a strange little rabbit that I discovered, many years later, from Sue Pearson, was Oswald the Lucky Rabbit, an early Disney character and forerunner of Mickey Mouse.

When I first bought Theo he had woollen eyes, stitched high up on his forehead, which gave him a very strange appearance. At the time, I thought he was earlier than he is as he has a pronounced hump. I therefore replaced the woollen eyes with boot buttons. Later, I realised that as he has rexine paws he must date from the thirties, at the earliest, and should have glass eyes. But by then I had got used to the boot-button look and it was too late to change his character.

Theo's character always seemed, to me, to be young and boyish. I began drawing him as a schoolboy before I actually made him his cap and blue felt blazer and cut down my old school tie.

My mother knitted him a little scarf and a pullover which was soon adorned with an accumulation of badges, his cycling proficiency badge taking pride of place. The pockets of his school blazer became obvious receptacles for such things as a miniature bar of chocolate, a tiny conker, his bus pass and savings book as well as various miniature pencils and tiny comics.

In 1991 Stacey Lee Terry of Bo-Bear Designs made a limited edition replica of Theo. She even had the school tie material specially made. He was sold in a box with his school report (not very exemplary) from Bo-Bears Academy, a bar of chocolate and bus pass in his pocket. There is a picture of the Theo replica in the Dorling Kindersley **Teddy Bear Encyclopedia**, in the section on Artist Bears.

As recounted earlier, Theo and the Colonel were close companions and, together with Jacko the monkey, got left on a London bus in 1994. The Colonel and Jacko have not been seen since but Theo came back to me, thanks to the television programme, Schofield's Quest. Phillip Schofield showed one of Stacey Lee Terry's replicas of Theo on the programme and recounted what had happened to the bears. He said that the replica would be offered in exchange for the real Theo and that there would be a monetary reward for the other two missing toys. Immediately after the show, someone telephoned the studio to say they had found Theo on his own. We were very excited when, the next day, Michael Hurll Television telephoned to say that the real Theo was there, in their office. I wanted to come up to London immediately to collect him but they asked if they could keep him until the next show, and sure enough, the following Sunday, the opening shot of the programme was little Theo sitting on a table in the television studio.

If we had had Sue Nicoll's replica of the Colonel at the time we might have got them both back. It was a great relief, though, to be at least reunited with Theo, still complete with school cap, chocolate and bus pass. Perhaps the bus pass was the clue to his return. The poor old Colonel only had his map of India.

Bingie Baby

Bingie Baby was made by Merrythought during the thirties as a toy especially for young children. He is very cuddly, being unjointed and made of very soft mohair. I acquired this little bear, together with a mixed assortment of furry friends, at a charity sale in the mid-eighties. After drawing him I regretfully sold him again but his character and baby looks have inspired various illustrations for children's books that I have done since.

Durban Ted

Durban Ted was one of the bears exhibited at the Arundel Toy and Military Museum before it closed. He started life in South Africa and acquired his fur coat and boots when he emigrated to England. He was one of the bears that I drew for the museum letterhead when the owner, Diana Henderson, commissioned me to design the museum stationery for her in the early eighties. There were some wonderful old bears in the museum, together with a large collection of interesting old toys, many of which I have drawn over the years. Sadly the museum is now closed and the collection has been dispersed.

Ted

Ted became known, first in his home country Australia and then in Britain, in the form of a book of exquisite drawings. **The Idle Bear** by Robert Ingpen, a much respected Australian artist, was published in Britain by Blackie and Son in 1986 and won the Hans Christian Andersen medal. Three years later it was published in a miniature version and was paired with a miniature edition of my book, **The Teddy Bears' Picnic**; they were presented together in a small counterpack in the shape of a hamper.

Ted is Robert Ingpen's childhood bear, having been given him by a great aunt at his birth in the mid-thirties. The name Ted is actually a nom de plume that was adopted on his becoming a literary bear, but to three generations of Ingpens he has always been known as Pooh. His companion, the Idle Bear, belongs to a childhood friend whose married name is Idle and was thus the inspiration for this first book. Ted has since appeared in several other teddy bear stories by Robert Ingpen.

Pooh (alias Ted) may be an all Australian bear as he has the broad forehead and wide-apart eyes of many of the early Joy-Toys. Joy-Toys, one of the first Australian teddy bear manufacturers, was founded in South Yarra, Victoria in the early twenties.

Heathcliffe and Jeff

Heathcliffe and Jeff are both Alpha Farnell bears dating from the thirties. I drew them in 1990 at the Cotswold Teddy Bear Museum in Broadway which was, at that time, owned by Wendy and Colin Lewis and called Unique. Wendy and Colin Lewis, having recently acquired some nice Farnell bears, suggested that I should come and draw them, and it was arranged that my husband and I should call in on our way back from a trip to Devon. On the day in question we headed up the motorway from Exeter and got caught in a dreadful traffic jam. It was extremely hot. We sat and stewed for about three hours and eventually arrived at the museum at about six o'clock in the evening. The Lewises were quite unperturbed and before we knew it we were being revived with large gins and tonics, overnight accommodation was fixed up with the B & B next door and I was comfortably settled in their museum, drawing teddy bears.

Unique closed in 1994 but opened again under new ownership

in 1996 and has since been known as Broadway Bears and Dolls.

Teddy Colin

Teddy Colin was the childhood bear of Sylvia Willgoss, who was a designer for Dean's from 1952 to 1980. He is a Chiltern bear dating from 1932. Sylvia always used to call him Teddy until one day she realised that many children have two names. From then on, she secretly called him Teddy Colin. Throughout Sylvia's years of creativity Teddy Colin has been a watchful companion, overseeing the designing and making of many wonderful toy animals. His wistful presence is well captured in the following lines of verse.

My Old Teddy

When we were young and new, Ted,
And both of us were small;
When a bear had hair,
And a brown-eyed stare,
When make-believe was all

Then you sat near my bed, Ted,
Your glass eyes watched my sleep;
With a brown-eyed stare,
When a bear had hair,
And a voice so growly deep.

Your growler is long dead, Ted,
And glass eyes lack the brown;
Now you're a bald eared bear,
With a pale-eyed stare,
Yet still you smile and never frown.

Sylvia Willgoss

Jock

Jock is also one of the great survivors. He is a real old veteran panda and started life in Exeter. When his young owner discovered that the family were going out to India, and that India was a very hot country, she kindly shaved the fur off his head and back to help him cope with the heat.

Thanks to the foresight of his little owner he survived the heat. He also survived the war years in besieged Malta when their house was destroyed by a bomb, being thrown out of the dormitory window at an English girl's boarding school and finally having his pink knitted shorts torn off by a stray dog in Singapore. In spite of all these mishaps, he still retains his dignity and lives in serene retirement in Yorkshire.

A real giant panda first arrived at Chicago Zoo in 1937. This was followed the next year by the arrival of Ming at London Zoo. The pandas became firm favourites with young and old and it was not long before all the leading teddy bear manufacturers were producing little black and white teddies. Toy pandas were naturally, and unquestionably, accepted amongst the teddy bear fraternity from the first, but it was not until 1988 that Dr Robert Hoage of the National Zoological Park in Washington DC officially declared the giant panda a member of the bear family.

Marcus

Marcus dates from 1938 and is possibly of Merrythought origins. I discovered him at Pollock's Toy Museum many years ago. At some stage in his life a loving owner had kitted him out with a smart, striped dressing gown, silk pyjamas and his own toothbrush. Sadly, although so well equipped, he languished for forty-five years in Harrods' Repository before his arrival at the museum. Perhaps the nightwear had been specially provided for his dark nights in storage, but one is left wondering about the untold story of why he was left there for so long.

I was very sorry to find, on a recent visit to Pollock's Toy Museum, that he was no longer on display but back in storage, down in the museum's basement. So poor old Marcus, like Rip van Winkle, is destined to slumber on. I am glad that he still has his dressing gown, but wish the museum staff would dress him in his silk pyjamas, as I am sure he would then sleep more comfortably.

English chain-store bear

Chapter Five

1940-1950

The years of the Second World War were traumatic for so many children all over Europe. It does not take much to imagine what solace the presence of a beloved and trusted bear would have given to those caught up in this world of chaos, bereavement and fear.

I remember as a small child seeing hordes of evacuee children at one of the main London railway stations. The children had labels tied to them and many clutched a bear or other cherished possession. The sight filled me with fear as I did not know where they were going or what was to become of them. Little did I know then that my future husband could have been amongst them and that they were, in theory, being given the opportunity of a quiet rural sojourn away from the dangers of bomb-torn London.

Teddy Bear Gas-mask Case

his case with a teddy bear head and appliquéed body is made of barage balloon material and was probably produced by one of the teddy bear factories whose machines were now working towards the war effort.

The dreaded gas-masks that we had to carry everywhere during the war years were another fear for the young. My little brother was terrified at the sight of his red "Mickey Mouse" gas-mask with its funny nose, which was standard issue for younger children. If it had come with a jolly little teddy bear case, like this one in the Petersfield Museum, I am sure he would have been a lot happier.

Beartrice

Beartrice is a home-made bear and she is very typical of the immediate post-war period when everything was scarce or cost precious ration coupons. Consequently there was a surge of make-do ingenuity and creativity, especially where toys were concerned. There were many bears like Beartrice produced from old blankets, some made from patterns published in magazines, and some strange-shaped amateur efforts of unique design. Beartrice wears her carefully knitted dress like a statement – "I may be home-made but I **am** properly dressed." I have drawn her here sitting on my mother's old identity card which she, like everyone else, had to carry in those days.

Bertie Beertje

Bertie Beertje is probably a Dutch bear. He is large and very solidly built and has flat plastic googly eyes and round floppy ears. He is made of artificial silk plush, in what was once a very bright golden-yellow colour.

*One of my daughters was a photography student at the art school in Rotterdam in the early eighties and used to send me wonderful postcards of Dutch teddies photographed by Mirja de Vries. She also bought me a copy of Mirja's book, **de Knuffels**, produced with Paul Haenen in 1980. Sadly, though, as the text is in Dutch I can only enjoy the pictures.*

Arnelda's Bear

Arnelda's Bear was purchased in America in 1944 and was probably made by Gund. It was originally bought for a much longed-for first grandchild but tragically neither the baby nor its mother survived the birth. The devastated grandparents later gave the bear to their daughter-in-law's first child and it has remained with her ever since. This little bear discovered at quite an early age that he could stand on his head and has spent most of his life viewing the world upside-down. He posed for me in this position without a single wobble.

Bruce

During the Second World War there was a general shortage of traditional bear-making materials. As a result sheepskin bears, both jointed and unjointed, were produced by manufacturers in the Antipodes and also in Britain. Some were dyed to the more usual teddy bear colours of gold, brown or black but many, like Bruce, were left white and looked more like sheep than bears.

Bruce is a sheepskin bear from Australia. He reminds me of a bear an aunt brought back from Sydney for my young brother at the end of the Second World War. We thought of him very much as alien stock with his tight, white, unyielding fleece and rather stiff unjointed limbs. He never made the inner royal circle and would lie around disconsolately, always on the edge of things.

Koala Lumpa

Koala Lumpa is a Chad Valley koala dating from the early fourties. His colour and British label deny any pretence of an Australian upbringing and he has obviously never smelt a gum tree in his life. He has, as a consequence, always suffered from a serious identity problem.

I have often included Koala Lumpa in my books with Theo and the Colonel. But I have had to use a good deal of artistic licence when drawing his very short arms and legs, as they would really hamper his style when competing with the other teddy bear characters.

The koala is, as everyone knows, a marsupial and therefore completely unrelated to the bear family. However, its cuddly image and quirky character endeared it to the teddy bear fraternity from the start. There is a story, probably apocryphal, that in 1880 King Edward VII took a fancy to a small koala that had just arrived at London Zoo and that from then on Koalas became accepted as teddy bears.

Willbear

Willbear was given to me by a friend who said his name was William Shakesbear. He did not strike me as being a bear with any particular literary leanings and his name soon became abbreviated to Willbear. He is a typical Chad Valley bear of this period, slightly tubby with a happy smiling face. He is always a willing model and I have drawn him in many different poses and situations. He looks like a bear who would enjoy the odd toffee (or three or four) so I have shown him here in sticky indulgence holding an old Macintosh's toffee tin.

Héloïse

Héloïse is a very sweet little French bear made of pink "art silk" which had been a favourite material since its introduction in 1929. I have drawn her treating two other little bears, Blanche and McLavender, to some patisserie. I bought Héloïse during a visit to Normandy, to the Club des Amis de l'Ours. It was a wonderfully warm, sunny weekend in early May. Marcelle Goffin had invited me over to France to give a talk at the club's reunion, being held that year at the Château de Fleury-la-Forêt deep in the woods near Rouen. The château houses a fine collection of dolls and old toys and the owners had invited the club to mount their own exhibition of teddy bears for the reunion.

My husband and I spent a delightful two days meeting many French bear makers, collectors and dealers. Héloïse will always be a reminder of that lovely weekend when we learned a great deal about French bears and, above all, enjoyed some wonderful Gallic hospitality.

A Group of small Japanese bears

Chapter Six

1950-1960

Teddy

eddy is a Tru-to-Life brown bear by Dean's. One of a series of lifelike toy animals designed by Sylvia Willgoss who was Dean's chief designer until the Rye factory closed in 1980.

I first met this bear when judging at a charity teddy bear event in Bexhill many years ago. No one, not even the Christie's expert, could throw any light on the age or origins of this ursine oddity with rubber mask and paws. I thought it was of particular interest and wrote down the owner's name and telephone number and asked if I could come and draw him at a later date. In 1990 when visiting Unique, the Cotswold Teddy Bear Museum, Wendy Lewis showed me a black Dean's Tru-to-Life bear that she had just bought and it was only then that I realised the identity of the Bexhill bear.

Recently I found the owner's name and telephone number that I had scribbled in my sketchbook many years previously. Luckily, she was still at the same address and remembered my interest in her bear and kindly let me draw him. She told me that an elderly neighbour had bequeathed Teddy to her in her will when she was a small child in 1959. She said that as Teddy had been in poor condition since she had first known him, she had assumed he was of a much

I later met Sylvia Willgoss who described being sent to London Zoo to do drawings of the animals for the Tru-to-Life series. The first animals she drew were the chimpanzees who were perfect models, but when it came to drawing the bears it was a different story. She told me that she was taken down a dark passage behind the Mappin Terraces and left on her own, tentatively clutching her sketchbook and pencils. There was a door at the back of the bears' inner sanctum, with a very small window quite high up. She stood on tip-toe and just managed to get a glimpse of a large bear-like shape silhouetted against the dim light. She had just stepped back from the window when suddenly a large paw with very long claws was thrust through the small opening. This unnerved her so much that she beat a hasty retreat.

Eventually, when the first brown Tru-to-Life bear cubs were produced, Dean's held a press launch at London Zoo. The photographs which appeared subsequently in the newspapers show the real bear cubs playing with the toy bears and it is impossible to tell which are which.

earlier date. In fact, he could only have been a few years old when the elderly neighbour died.

As Teddy is very much a member of the family she asked me to draw him holding his rather sad little companion which belongs to her son, now a young adult and off travelling the world.

Sooty

Sooty first appeared on children's television in the early fifties. His creator, Harry Corbet, had bought the little glove puppet in 1948 from an old lady who used to sell her home-made bears on Blackpool pier. Harry, who was a part-time children's entertainer, blackened the bear's ears and nose and named him Sooty. Sooty was soon incorporated into Harry's magic show and he was later invited to fill a regular slot on children's television. It was not long before Sooty became known and loved by children all over the world. Chad Valley were granted the merchandising rights and soon little Sooty glove puppets were a common sight.

When I first started buying old bears they often had ears or limbs missing. In those days bear making as a hobby was non-existent so it was not possible to buy the right kinds of material for bear repairs. I asked the advice of a friend who had a shop selling old dolls and toys and she produced a couple of Sooty glove puppets and said they were what she used. I bought the two puppets, very cheaply, but have never had the heart to cut them up and cannibalise them in the way she suggested. I perched them on the top of my easel where they have remained to this day, except when taken down to entertain grandchildren.

Teddy Robinson

The Teddy Robinson stories were great favourites of my children when they were young. The gently told, everyday adventures of Deborah and her teddy bear conjure up a cosy and unthreatening world. Therefore, when I was compiling my anthology Teddy Robinson was high on the list for inclusion. I had heard that Deborah was Joan Robinson's daughter and that she still had her teddy.

So I wrote to the publisher to see if they would put me in touch with the family. Unfortunately, at the time I wrote, Joan Robinson was in hospital following a stroke. Harrap put me in touch with Deborah, though, who confirmed that Teddy Robinson was still very much a part of the family but that I would have to get permission from her mother to do the drawing.

Eventually I received an invitation to tea to meet Joan Robinson and the famous little bear. When Deborah showed me into the house Teddy Robinson was immediately recognisable from the pen and ink drawings of him in the books. I was charmed to meet Joan Robinson, as well as her daughter, Deborah, and each of the third generation of the family as they returned home from school.

We discussed whether I should draw Teddy Robinson as he is now, with one eye missing, or with both eyes in place. It was eventually decided that as one of his adventures was about losing an

Now, nearly fifty years on, the **Teddy Robinson** *books are all still in print and delighting new generations of children.*

eye it would be appropriate to draw him as he really was. Joan told me that most of the stories had been based on real life situations and Deborah got out the family photograph albums to prove it.

It was a very happy afternoon and a memory that I will treasure, especially as Joan sadly died after another stroke, before the anthology was published. I felt privileged that I had been able to meet her and enjoy an afternoon in the close ambience of the three generations of the family and their much loved little bear.

Max

Max is a Hermann bear dating from the fifties. He has a date ? 5.57 marked on his foot. I do not know what the date signifies as I have only recently acquired him, but it is very likely the date he was bought, or perhaps it marks the date of a birth and he was some lucky baby's first teddy bear. The open mouth is very much a feature of German bears, the most well known being the Zotty bears which Steiff introduced at about the same time.

Senior Under Officer Edward Bear

Senior Under Officer Edward Bear was the proud mascot for the Sandhurst Royal Military Academy Parachute Club, which was founded in 1950. His uniform was made by Moss Bros. and his parachute, also an exact miniature replica, was made by the RAF Parachute School in Abingdon. He has various badges and wings stitched to his uniform, all of which have been earned, and a log book that reports every drop he has taken part in.

Shortly after I drew this portrait of him in 1987 it was decided that he deserved retirement, having completed over four hundred jumps and, as a consequence, suffered multiple injuries – all in the call of duty. He now resides in the Royal Military Academy Museum and his place has been taken by a younger bear.

Edward II, the new Parachute Club mascot, is a Merrythought Yes/No bear and was bought at Harrods. One wonders whether when it comes to hurtling out of an aircraft at 240m, young Edward ever considers his yes/no option. Somehow I doubt it, as he already has a reputation for being a bold and willing bear and a fitting replacement for his brave namesake.

Celeste

Celeste is a small, 16cm high Jean-Pierre Massy bear that I recently found in a Paris flea market. She is a very typical little French bear with her pink-lined ears and very upturned nose. She wears a nappy tied with a piece of pink ribbon and a bit of cut-down smocking for a dress. I could imagine some small French child in the fifties dressing her and playing with her. I have been informed, though, that French bear collectors do not approve of bears in clothing, which is interesting for a country that one associates so much with fashion.

Jason

Jason is one of the original designs of this well-loved character bear, first produced by Merrythought in 1957 and named Cheeky. With his cute expression and over-sized ears, each containing a bell, he has proved to be one of the classics of the teddy bear world. Merrythought have since introduced other variations of the original character, all with the same broad grin and large ears that are his hallmark. I drew this little bear from Pat Rush's collection. Pat has always had a particular interest in Merrythought bears and is extremely knowledgeable about them and many other aspects of the teddy bear world.

*I first met Pat in 1988 when she wrote an article about me for the American magazine **Teddy Bear and Friends**, which was eventually published in December 1989. Pat was then living in St Leonards and was one of the first actual teddy bear collectors that I had met. She kindly allowed me to come round and draw some of the bears in her collection and since then has always been most helpful with my many questions and queries.*

Lefray Bear

Lefray Bear is another of Sue Pearson's bears who appears in one of my sketchbooks. Teddy bears produced by some of the lesser-known British factories have attracted more attention in recent years; much more is now known about these less familiar names of teddy bear genealogy.

Lefray Toys Ltd were established in 1948 in West London. They moved to larger premises in St Albans in Hertfordshire in 1960, which enabled them to increase their output substantially. They later moved to South Wales and in 1990 obtained the licence to produce Rupert Bear.

Frau Zimt

Frau Zimt is a small German bear. She is well made, in warm reddish-brown velvet. Her eyes are little jet beads, and probably not original. Her colour reminds me of Christmas time in Germany and the accompanying smells of cinnamon and spices. I have, therefore, depicted Frau Zimt cooking. This is also an excuse to draw a little tin range bought from one of my favourite shops, Die Puppenstube in Valentinskamp, Hamburg. This shop stocks every accessory a small bear could dream about and is a complete Mecca for anyone with a weakness for things miniature.

Audrey

Audrey is a sad little bear, but typical of the fifties. She has a cloth body with a synthetic plush head and paws, and fixed yellow felt boots. She was an unexpected addition to my collection in 1993. My dear friend, Anna Awdry, died early that summer and sadly I was not able to go to her funeral. Afterwards I got a surprise parcel from Audrey Duck, of Good Bears of the World, containing this rather dishevelled pink bear. Apparently at the funeral there was a large box, filled with Anna's bears, placed at the back of the church. Everyone had been invited to take home a bear in memory of Anna. I was very touched that Audrey thought of me and took the trouble to take a bear for me and send it. Sad little bear that she is, she nonetheless encapsulates so much of Anna who was an immensely caring person. She had a very large collection of bears, many of whom were waifs and strays that many another collector would not have given house-room. to Because of the Awdry/Audrey associations the bear has inevitably become known as Audrey.

Hessel

*H*essel, made in 1959, was the first bear created by Naomi Laight. I first became aware of Naomi's bears in the early eighties when I used to attend various antique toy and teddy bear fairs. There were very few makers of new teddy bears around in those days and Naomi's were very distinctive. They were usually made in different coloured chenille plush and were the first quality modern bears that I had seen. I have followed her progress with interest ever since.

Hessel was Naomi's first ever youthful attempt at making a teddy bear. It came about because her grandmother had recently died and she felt a need to create a memento of her. She decided that this memento should take the form of a teddy bear and that she would make it out of her grandmother's fur cape. When the bear was finished, she decided to call him Hessel, after her grandfather.

Two little Polish bears

Chapter Seven
1960-1970

Pteddy

Pteddy started life as a fluffy little blue and yellow Wendy Boston bear. He belongs to my son who was born in West Africa on the 60th anniversary, to the day, of the first appearance of Clifford Berryman's famous cartoon in the **Washington Post**. Our son took his time to make his entrance into the world, and friends who were returning to England before the happy event left the little bear for him. So, throughout a protracted labour, I had Pteddy for company together with a very large, very green, praying mantis that insisted on sitting on the end of the bed regarding us both with a quizzical expression.

Our son showed us from an early age that he was destined to become a historian and his toys were constantly caught up in historical re-enactments. Pteddy acquired the P prefix to his name during an Egyptian period, when he spent days and nights buried under a pyramid of bricks. This probably accounts for his somewhat mummified appearance today.

Wendy Boston was a toy manufacturer who started producing soft toys in the immediate post-war years. They pioneered "play safe" toys, setting initial standards which were the forerunners of the EU directives of today. They invented machine washable teddy bears with safety, screw-locked, plastic eyes which revolutionised the toy industry of the time. Under the label Wendy Boston Playsafe Toys Limited they became one of the leading British teddy bear manufacturers until the factory closed in 1976, having been acquired in 1968 by Denys Fisher and then latterly by Palitoy. I can certainly vouch for the machine washability and also the safety-lock eyes which are Pteddy's only feature that have never had to be repaired.

Zotty

Zotty Teddy was given to his owner in the mid-sixties and eighteen years later accompanied him to Oxford to read medicine. As the college in question was St Edmund Hall, known in undergraduate circles as Teddy Hall, there were quite a few teddy bears in attendance. This teddy sat his finals with his owner, wearing his own mortar board, obligatory for anyone sitting exams at Oxford. I was first asked to do a portrait of him with his mortar board as a memento of the occasion and perhaps too as a reminder of his student "salad days". He now lives with his owner and family in America.

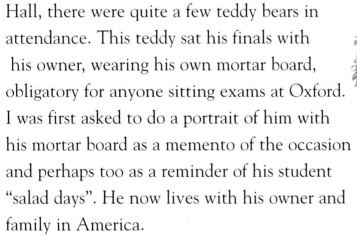

The Steiff, open-mouthed, Zotty bears were first introduced in 1951 and are now a firmly established classic. The name is derived from the German word Zottelig, meaning shaggy.

Hawthorn

Hawthorn is the only bear that I have ever made. Touched by appeals from my two-year-old daughter that she did not have a teddy bear, I decided that I would make her one. We were living in a fairly remote corner of northern Nigeria at the time, far from any shops that sold the usual commodities. I therefore had to make a teddy using local resources and my own initiative. The stuffing was the easiest part as we were surrounded by fields of cotton and tall kapok trees. It was not difficult to obtain cotton waste from the local ginning factory, and kapok could be gathered from the pods of the silk cotton trees. We often had wonderful "snow storms" when the wind would burst the long brown pods with resounding cracks and the kapok would blow out, covering everything with a fine silky dusting of white fluff.

I am not particularly proud of my creation. He is large and floppy, his ears are too big and his eyes too small, but my daughter loved him at first sight. With a two-year-old's determination and some kind of mysterious agenda of her own she christened him Hawthorn, and with that name he is now an accepted member of the family. The duffel coat was made for his final return to Britain, and it has his name on a tape stitched to the lining. The bear, in his duffel coat with a miniature paintbox in the pocket, accompanied her to art school at Exeter many years later and nowadays he is usually to be found in her eldest daughter's bedroom.

Berlin Bear

This little bear, only 10cm tall, should have a small crown on his head, and would have been bought as a souvenir by tourists visiting Berlin in the sixties. He was made by the appropriately named maker, Karl Bär. In 1967 Karl bought a quantity of cheap plush from Italy and consequently won the contract to produce the souvenir Berlin Bears. These were manufactured under his name for the next fifteen years. The Karl Bär Company also bought Schuco from the receiver in 1977, and continued to make the miniature Piccolo series, having acquired all the patterns and metal components for the bears' bodies. The templates for the metal ears, however, were lost in the transfer. So Karl Bär manufactured their Piccolo bears with a wire frame for the ears instead. These bears were marketed under the name Heike-Bär. Heike being the name of Karl's wife.

Teddy Edward

Teddy Edward is a small Chiltern bear. He belonged to Sarah Matthews, and first rose to fame in a series of nineteen books written by her parents, Mollie and Patrick Matthews. They posed the bear in different locations and took black and white photographs of him to illustrate the stories. Later he became a television star appearing on Watch with Mother during the sixties and seventies. In a series of twelve films, narrated by Richard Baker, the little teddyjetted his way round the world. He was shown in exotic locations such as Timbuktu, Mount Everest and the Grand Canyon, always with his little red suitcase and silver medal, won in a skiing competition.

In 1989 I received a surprise Christmas card from Teddy Edward saying how much he had enjoyed seeing all his friends in my anthology, but he was very sad that he had not been included. I wrote back assuring him that I would include a drawing of him in the next book. Sadly, by the time an appropriate opportunity had arisen Patrick Matthews had died and Teddy Edward, together with his suitcase, medal and many other related items, had been sold at Christie's for the amazing sum of £34,500.

The buyer was Mr Sekiguchi of the Sun Arrow Toy Company, and owner of Teddy Girl. Teddy Edward is now in another of Mr Sekiguchi's museums at Nasu, 100km north of Tokyo. Well, Teddy Edward, this is just to let you know that I have fulfilled my promise. So I hope you will manage to see this drawing and feel placated at last.

Toffee

offee was a popular character from the BBC radio Listen With Mother programme which was enjoyed by many small children during the fifties. This little Toffee bear was produced by Farnell in the mid-sixties when the business had moved to Hastings. He is shown in their 1968 catalogue wearing his little red hat and scarf and is offered in either a white or toffee colour, 30cms high, together with a free story book.

Also shown in the same catalogue is Coney Bear, *"The Father of them all – with growl"*. This bear was made in varying sizes from 12cms to 50cms and was selected by the Council for Industrial Design for the Design Centre, London.

Chad Valley also produced a Toffee Bear in 1953.

Henrietta

Chapter Eight

1970-1980

Odd and Elsewhere

The seventies were lean years where bears were concerned. The traditional teddy bears that had been the lead sellers for most of the toy manufacturers during the past six decades were now ousted by cheap, flat-faced relatives from Korea, China and Taiwan. Several respected teddy bear makers, Farnell in particular, did not survive. Sadly, if they had only known that a great teddy bear revival was just around the corner they might have kept going long enough to enjoy a rebirth in the nineties, as happened to Dean's.

Odd and Elsewhere, a small teddy bear and a clown doll, were the invention of James Roose-Evans in the seventies. He wrote seven books about the toys, who were inseparable comrades in a series of exciting adventures. In the stories the toys' home is Fenton House in Hampstead, owned by the National Trust. There is now an Odd and Elsewhere room in the house where

you can see the original toys that appear in the books, together with various bits of memorabilia.

When I drew Odd and Elsewhere they were still in James Roose-Evans' flat. I had arranged a time with him when it would be convenient to come and draw the toys. I arrived at the appointed time, pressed the doorbell and a warm rich voice on the remote answering device invited me to come in and to climb the stairs till I could go no further. It was a long climb and the stairs became narrower and darker but I could hear some Mozart coming from somewhere higher up, which

encouraged me to continue. At last at the top, I found myself at a door that was being held open by the tall figure of James Roose-Evans himself. He ushered me in and introduced me to the toys. I was surprised and delighted to find that as well as Odd and Elsewhere there were other lovely old toys, on which James had based his characters of Collander Moll and Hallelujah Jones, the latter being a wonderful old Steiff doll with huge feet.

James fetched a tray of tea and invited me to make myself at home. He said that he was sorry that he had to go out but I could stay and draw as long as I liked and let myself out when I had finished. So, with a nice cup of tea, and Mozart for company, I had a relaxed and undisturbed drawing session. How different to my encounter with Teddy Girl in Edinburgh!

Peter Bull's Bears

These three bears were drawn from a collection of Peter Bull's bears that were on display at the London Toy and Model Museum before it closed. The one on the left is a Bully Bear, created by Alison Wilson for the House of Nisbet. Bully Bear, inspired by Delicatessen was the main character in a series of six little books that were published in the early eighties. They were written by Peter Bull and illustrated by Enid Irving.

Paddington

Paddington is one of the most well-known and best-loved teddy bear characters in the world today, second only to Winnie-the-Pooh. He was the creation of the writer Michael Bond who wrote the first Paddington story in 1958.

This is the first Paddington toy bear made by Shirley Clarkson who was the creative force behind Gabrielle Designs. He was donated to The National Toy Museum in Rottingdean, near Brighton, in 1972 and it was here that I drew him in the early eighties. The museum at Rottingdean is no longer owned by Brighton and Hove Borough Council, and the toys and teddy bears that were on show there are at present in storage. It is hoped that eventually they will be displayed at Hove Museum.

In the first Paddington stories, with their wonderfully lively illustrations by Peggy Fortnum, Paddington does not wear boots. When Shirley was designing the first Paddington toy bear she gave him boots so that he would be able to stand up. The boots are now such an integral part of the Paddington character it is difficult to imagine him without them. I have discovered over the years that whenever I have done a design showing a bear in boots people tend to say, "Oh, Paddington!" even when the bear shows no likeness whatsoever to Michael Bond's famous character.

Reverend Bear

Reverend Bear is an American teddy bear. He was a gift from the Altar Guild of St Ambrose Episcopal Church in the Claremont diocese of Los Angeles to their British rector while he was there on an exchange visit in 1976. The exchange had been arranged as part of the two-hundredth birthday celebrations of the United States.

Alresford Crafts was founded by Margaret and John Jones in 1970 in the Town Mill at Alresford in Hampshire. Margaret designed a wide range of soft toy animals which were exported worldwide, but by the early eighties it was the teddy bears that had become their main product. John Jones died in 1991 and Margaret closed the business in 1992.

Prince

Prince is a large golden-coloured bear with velvety fur. It was made by Alresford Crafts in the late seventies and was bought for my brother's first-born when he was about five years old. As my brother's bear, King, was still keeping an aged eye on the nursery, Prince was the obvious name for this new youngster.

American Carrousel bear

Chapter Nine

1980-1990

Yetta

Yetta, short for Yetta Nother Bear, was the first mohair bear made by Carol-Lynn Rössel Waugh in 1985. She was one of a group of pioneering bear artists in America, known for her writing and talks on the subject. Carol-Lynn was also one of the first to introduce the term bear artist – one who designs and makes bears. (As opposed to people, like me, who draw them and should be called bear illustrators to avoid confusion!) Carol-Lynn came from a background of doll making and began experimenting with porcelain and latex bears in the mid-seventies, eventually producing her first mohair teddy bears ten years later.

I met Carol-Lynn in 1993 when Margaret and Gerry Grey organised a Teddy Bear Convention in Northampton. Many American teddy bear artists had been invited over for it and this was the first time that I really became aware of this new ursine breed – the artist bear. The bears made by British bear makers that I had seen up until then were based very much on the traditional teddy. These bears, though, were something very different and were far removed from the cosy concept of a nursery toy. They were personal artistic interpretations, made by adults for adults.

Some were wackily outrageous and I felt totally bewildered by the whole thing.

Carol-Lynn gave a very good presentation on the work of American bear artists and introduced us to many of their somewhat alien creations. She explained the reason and inspiration for many of the bears and I began to understand something of the phenomenon. Now, since the mid-nineties, artist bears, as opposed to antique bears, appear to have become the dominant focus of teddy bear collecting worldwide.

Mo Bear

Mo Bear was one of a group of bears made by Sylvia Willgoss after she was made redundant when Dean's moved from Rye in 1980. Sylvia always says that she is a wildlife artist rather than a teddy bear artist and most of the freelance toys she has made in her post-Dean's years are small woodland creatures, all beautifully researched and made to a very high standard.

Harry

Harry is the smallest of the Burberry bear family. In 1987 I was commissioned by the well-known clothes store in London's Haymarket to write a children's book based on the Burberry bears, made exclusively for their children's department by Merrythought.

I wrote and illustrated a story called **The Very Special Party** in which I incorporated all the Burberry bears, Ben, Victoria, Thomas, Annabelle, Emily and Harry, two Burberry rag dolls, Laura and Clare, and my own old teddy, Theo. I set the book in the then children's department, which was upstairs in the Haymarket shop, and drew the toys wearing children's clothes from the Burberry range. At the time I was writing the book there was also an exhibition of vintage Burberry raincoats on show at the Victoria & Albert Museum which proved further inspiration.

The story that was eventually published was about a grand party to which all the toys had been invited. Poor old Theo, though, has nothing suitable to wear. So the kind Burberry bears kit him out in a smart jacket from the shop. Unfortunately, on the day of the party, it pours with rain. The Burberry bears have plenty of smart raincoats and umbrellas, but they are concerned about Theo, whom they have arranged to meet at the party venue. Theo, however, turns up with his new jacket well protected by a vintage Burberry raincoat which, he announces proudly, he has had all his life – a good fifty years.

The book was published in 1988 and sold through the Burberry shops worldwide. The Managing Director of Burberry's Retail presented me with Harry as a thank you.

The Very Special Party *was reprinted in 1998 for a special promotion in Japan to mark Burberry's one hundred and fiftieth*

Benjamin, Henry and Fritz

Benjamin, Henry and Fritz were created by Carol Ann Stanton. Like many other people with bear interests, Carol came from a background of doll making, as is very obvious when meeting these funny little characters. Their somewhat hedgehog-like faces and peasant clothes give the impression that they have just emerged from the Black Forest or straight out of the pages of Grimms' Fairy Tales.

The Professor

The Professor is an American bear that I won in a raffle. In June 1990 Hugglets organised an event for Teddy Bear Club members to meet Doris and Terry Michaud and a party of thirty American bear lovers who were visiting Brighton. We were invited to bring along a British teddy bear, old if possible, so my husband and I went along accompanied by Theo, who was certainly old and British. During the evening The Professor, a Carrousel bear made by the Michauds was raffled to the British party and to my utmost surprise I was the lucky winner. The Professor was one of the first new bears in my collection and I was delighted to acquire him. He is beautifully made and has proved to be very drawable over the years, usually masquerading in other clothes.

There is a drawing of him on the title page for this chapter, not with his familiar spectacles and knitted cardigan, but as the transatlantic visitor that he is, with accompanying pieces of luggage. These are, in fact, old biscuit tins and part of yet another, unintended, collection.

Theo also enjoyed the evening and made many new friends. Amongst them was a Canadian bear lover from Quebec who corresponded with me for many years afterwards. Theo still wears a little Canadian badge on his pullover, presented to him that evening. When the replica Theo was available, number eight of the edition emigrated to Canada in a cardboard box. He seems to enjoy the Canadian way of life but, sadly, the school reports that continued to be sent back home for a while showed a marked deterioration in his school work.

Lakeland Bear

*I*n 1989 Wendy Phillips, a knitwear designer, advertised a small jumper using a Little Folk teddy bear as a model. She was immediately inundated with requests from teddy bear enthusiasts wanting to buy similarly dressed bears. Thus, Lakeland Bears was born, and proved so successful that the Phillips opened a shop in Bowness-on-Windermere where the range rapidly expanded.

The bears soon acquired the full hill-walking gear, including wonderful, stout, north country clogs, specially made for them. I remember meeting Wendy and her daughter at the Spring Fair in Birmingham in 1990. I had dressed one of my bears in climbing clothes for the launch of my book, **The Great Expedition**. Wendy was intrigued to know where I had found a miniature pair of climbing boots. Unfortunately there was only one, the other foot was subtly hidden in the display. I had found the little boot, appropriately enough, at a boot fair. It was in the form of a pincushion souvenir from Switzerland. Once I had picked out the pincushion padding I had a perfect little climbing boot, but sadly only one.

McSteiff

McSteiff is an Atlantic bear from Gairloch in the Scottish Highlands, made by Wendy and Alan Mullaney. I bought him in 1989 after meeting relatives of the Mullaneys while exhibiting at the Highland Gift Fair at Aviemore. We were told that Wendy and Alan had begun making bears with long snouts and humpbacks, similar to the early Steiff bears. However, having made them, they were not sure how to set about marketing them. After the fair we wrote to Wendy and Alan enclosing a copy of the 1989 UK Teddy Bear Guide and suggested they should be listed for the following year. We also asked if they could send us information about their bears. We soon received photographs of their small,

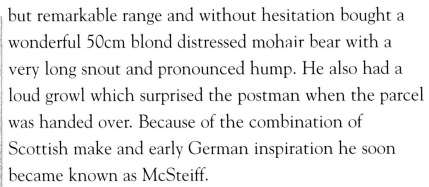

but remarkable range and without hesitation bought a wonderful 50cm blond distressed mohair bear with a very long snout and pronounced hump. He also had a loud growl which surprised the postman when the parcel was handed over. Because of the combination of Scottish make and early German inspiration he soon became known as McSteiff.

Readers may be puzzled that I have referred to McSteiff as "he" but have drawn him wearing a dress! I have found that most toys, especially bears, are not too concerned about questions of gender and they have all posed for me at different times wearing a variety of clothes. I have a complete wardrobe that belonged to a family doll dating from 1910. The clothes fit McSteiff very well, in spite of his large hump and long arms, and he is always happy to model them for me.

This is another drawing of McSteiff, showing him this time in masculine attire. I have drawn him here accompanied by Mark Anthony whose turn it was to do the cross-dressing.

The UK Teddy Bear Guide *was first published by Hugglets in October 1987 and has been produced annually ever since. It is a mine of information on all things teddy.*

Merrythought and Gund

Chapter Ten

1990-2002

Berry Branigan

The nineties were the years of the artist bear. Previously, mohair had only been available in 30m rolls which, being expensive, led to large editions and few bear makers. Now, for the first time, mohair became available in short lengths and in a greater variety of colours and styles. This inspired smaller editions and many special one-off creations. Many erstwhile collectors now turned their hands to designing their own bears and a growing creative force became unleashed, not only in America and Europe but also in Australia and the Far East.

Berry Branigan is a small, appealing bear made in a limited edition of one hundred and fifty by Stacey Lee Terry of Bo-Bear Designs in 1990. Stacey had called the edition Branigan but I added the Berry because of his black beady eyes. This was the second of the very few, new bears I have ever bought; I always say I am not a collector although somehow I seem to have amassed quite a large motley collection over the years. I have drawn the little bear here sitting beside a doll that I discovered in pieces in the attic of our previous house. She had a very sweet face, sadly broken. I spent many happy hours mending and dressing her and making her little boots from an old leather glove. My daughters were delighted with the final result and called her Sophie.

Several people had suggested to me that I should get a limited edition of Theo made and I had been assessing the work of various British bear makers with this in mind. When I discovered Stacey's bears I knew that my search was at an end and I commissioned Bo-Bears to undertake the making of a two hundred and fifty limited edition of Theo bears. Stacey spared no effort in her attention to detail with the replica, especially with his school uniform, even getting his tie and cap badge specially woven. The limited edition replica of Theo was finally launched in 1991 and, as recounted in a previous chapter, proved instrumental in getting the original Theo back to me after he went AWOL on a London bus in 1994.

Plume

Plume is a very sweet little 20cm French bear made by Marcelle Goffin under the label Ours de Marcelle. Marcelle has been the driving force behind recent research into French teddy bear manufacturers. Very little was known about early French bears until Marcelle retired and decided to fill her time trying to find out more about the subject. Together with Marylou Jouet, one of France's first bear artists, she formed Teddy's Patch, a group for French bear lovers. The group's newsletter, **Teddy's Flash,** is a lively publication containing much information on French bears, both old and new, and the group now has members all over France.

A teddy bear in France is usually simply called un ours (often abbreviated to the childish term nounours). Wendy Boston, advertising her famous washable bears in 1960, playfully states, "In France a bear is ours." But now, thanks to the research achieved by Marcelle and her group, we know that there would have been at least twenty-five French bear manufacturers competing with her.

Barnaby B. Bear

Barnaby B. Bear is a little Boyds Bear. I have been a great admirer of The Boyds Collection since first discovering them in 1991. I was therefore delighted when, in 1995, I was approached by Pinky Daniel, past President of the Florida State Association of Porcelain Artists. Pinky asked for permission to replicate some of my illustrations from my book of **The Teddy Bears' Picnic** on a miniature tea-set. Permission was granted and eventually a wonderful parcel arrived from Florida containing the prototype. The tea-set was beautifully presented in a willow basket, hand-made in Vermont, complete with padded lining and coverlet made in home-spun cotton by Mission Valley Textiles in Texas. A copy of **The Teddy Bears' Picnic** was also included, as well as a lucky little picnicker in the shape of Barnaby B. Bear, a delightful, jointed, bean-filled, Boyds bear. I have drawn him here, on the left, enjoying his picnic with a Canadian friend, chosen by my grandchildren, who were very happy to arrange the picnic spread for me.

The Boyds Collection Jointed Bean-Bag Teddy Bears were created by designer and bear artist Gae Sharp and were trade marked under the name J.B.Bean & Associates in 1985. Gae pioneered the jointed, bean-filled bear with the aim of making "A poseable bear that would hug back when hugged." The popularity that bean-filled bears have enjoyed since then has certainly proved that her instincts were right.

Mortimer, Martha, Max and Marigold

Mortimer, Martha, Max and Marigold are four bears that were created by Jaqueline Revitt for Merrythought in 1993. They were designed as Prue Theobalds' Character Bears for Merrythought's International Collectors Catalogue and were launched with an accompanying book. The book was called **The Bears' Seaside Adventure** and was a story about the four Merrythought bears coming to visit their cousins at the seaside. The seaside cousins were my bears, Theo, the Colonel, Koala Lumpa and McLavender. The book was sold by Merrythought with the bears, and also on general release. It is still in print, although the bears themselves sold out some time ago.

Alice and Mary

Alice and Mary are two little 15cm-high creations from the needle of Elaine Lonsdale. As with all Elaine's bears, the subtle use of textiles, lengths of antique ribbon, sprigs of velvet flowers and, above all, the wonderful hats are what make these, and many of her Companion Bears, so enchantingly different.

In December 1996 I was invited to open the new Broadway Bears Museum which had been bought by Janice Longhi from Wendy and Colin Lewis. There was a great party afterwards and it was here that I met Elaine and was introduced to my first Companion Bear. Elaine's bear making came out of her love of vintage clothes and old textiles. In 1987 she had opened a shop selling antique clothing and jewellery and also began collecting lace, hats, old hat pins and costume jewellery. With her love of textiles it is not surprising that all this led Elaine down the bear making path. And, of course, not only making them but dressing them and making hats and accessories for them from all the lovely materials she had gathered over the years. Colour, as well as texture, is very important to her and she often hand dyes fabric to get just the right effect. In this drawing Alice, on the left, is wearing a hand tinted coat and hat.

I was delighted to hear that one of Elaine's bears had won The Golden George at the Hennef fair in 1999.

Brodie Bear

B rodie Bear was commissioned in 1995 by the National Trust for Scotland from Sue Nicoll of Border Bruins. The idea for the bear came from Brodie Castle, one of the National Trust for Scotland's properties, where a nursery is one of the rooms on view to visitors. Once the bear was made, I was commissioned to produce a limited edition print which showed Brodie Castle with the bear in front and also some notelet packs depicting Brodie Bear playing golf and Brodie Bear playing the bagpipes. These were all sold at National Trust properties throughout Scotland.

Brodie is an engaging little bear with a rugged look, the colour and texture of highland cattle. One could imagine him on a remote mountainside looming out of the mist to the skirl of bagpipes.

Paul and Josef

P aul and Josef are "distressed" bears designed by the German teddy bear artist Werner Pyschny. They were made in a limited edition of one hundred for the Dortmund based company, Bear by Bear, as part of their Nostalgie Collection.

In 1993 I was approached by Helga and Manfred Schepp of Bear by Bear who had seen my drawings on various promotional material for Hugglets events in Britain. They liked these and asked me if I would design a logo for their company, which I was delighted to do. I was also pleased to create another logo in 1995 for a range of bears called Happy Bärli, designed by Helga, for Happy People, M. Klein GmbH in Bremen.

Blue Denim Bear

Blue Denim Bear is the creation of the German bear artist, Marie Robischon. I first saw Marie's bears in Germany in 1996 and was stunned, not only by the detail of the workmanship but above all by the characters. I had never seen bears like these before. There is nothing cute about Marie's characters. Many of them are dressed as bikers, punks, tramps, or wear uniforms of one kind or another, but each one is a painstakingly detailed individual with a life of its own. They look at you with their serious, close set, large black eyes and your attention is immediately caught as though about to engage in conversation.

Marie Robischon's bears are registered under the name Robin der Bär and many of them appear in an attractive book called **Robin der Bär (Robin the Bear)** *published in 1999 by Verlag Marianne Cieslik. The book is available in both German and English editions.*

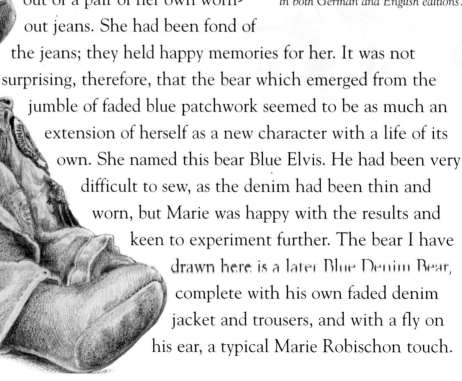

Marie made her first denim bear out of a pair of her own worn-out jeans. She had been fond of the jeans; they held happy memories for her. It was not surprising, therefore, that the bear which emerged from the jumble of faded blue patchwork seemed to be as much an extension of herself as a new character with a life of its own. She named this bear Blue Elvis. He had been very difficult to sew, as the denim had been thin and worn, but Marie was happy with the results and keen to experiment further. The bear I have drawn here is a later Blue Denim Bear, complete with his own faded denim jacket and trousers, and with a fly on his ear, a typical Marie Robischon touch.

Yona

ona is a beautifully realistic bear that I encountered in 1996 when he had just been nominated for a Toby Award. The following year, not surprisingly, he was winner of the British Bear Artist Award. The talented creator was Sandra Wickenden who has made a speciality of creating very realistic, multi-jointed bears.

Sandra told me that she first started making teddy bears in 1991 after having to leave her job as an accident and emergency nurse because of illness, and what started as a form of occupational therapy soon became a complete new way of life. It was Sandra's fascination with bears in the wild and the rôle they played in the history of the teddy bear that led her to study them. She was intrigued with the way that wild bears moved and she managed to make her bears replicate those movements by using multiple joints. The results are very successful and her bears are so life-like that you can almost sense their noses twitching.

Eisbär and Baby

E isbär and Baby are both Steiff bears and belong to Leon, a young German friend in Hamburg. Leon enjoys visiting the famous Hagenbeck Zoo where there are real polar bears. This zoo also has interesting links with Steiff, as Richard Steiff is purported to have sketched the performing bears from Carl Hagenbeck's touring animal circus. It was these sketches that were to inspire the pioneering jointed teddies which eventually made the Steiff name so famous.

Even before the first jointed bears, Steiff had introduced a pull-along polar bear on wheels, which is shown in their catalogue for 1897. Perhaps this too was inspired by one of Hagenbeck's polar bears.

Carl Hagenbeck's father had been a fish merchant in Hamburg and used to exhibit the seals that were caught in the fishing nets. In 1848, when Carl was just four years old, Herr Hagenbeck bought a polar bear that had been brought into port on a whaler. Gradually he collected a small menagerie of animals which Carl grew up with and eventually inherited in 1865. Carl was interested in training animals and pioneered methods of treating them with kindness and rewards. Hagenbeck's famous performing animals became well-known and popular throughout Europe. He is said to have brought a troupe of performing polar bears to the London Hippodrome in 1909. Hagenbeck's Zoo in Hamburg was opened in 1873 and was the first zoo designed to house animals in large buildings and to show them in as natural a state as possible.

Ambrosia and Snowy

Ambrosia and Snowy are two bears that were given to one of our granddaughters for her first Christmas. Ambrosia was a present from her aunt and is a soft and cuddly character without pedigree, but she is much loved, much cuddled and often used as a pillow. Snowy, on the other hand, was bought by me. He was specially selected from Deans as a classic bear that would accompany her through life and would hopefully survive to be passed down to her children in the time-honoured tradition of a loved and classic toy.

But, seeing Snowy always sitting sedately by himself, uncuddled, not played with and never taken to bed, I questioned her. "Don't you like Snowy?" I asked. "Well, put it this way," she said with all the wisdom of her seven years, "Ambrosia is the teddy I love now but Snowy is the one that I shall probably take to university."

Beanie Babies

Beanie Babies have proved to be the marketing phenomenon of the nineties. They were the brainchild of H. Ty Warner who set up his Ty Inc. Company in the United States in 1986. Initially Ty made high-quality soft toys for children, but produced some limited edition collector's bears in the early nineties. The Beanie Babies, a wide range of small, engaging animals, were introduced to the range in 1993 as cheap pocket money toys for children. A series of little Beanie bears were added in the 1994 catalogue and gradually the popularity of these little collectibles gathered momentum. By 1996 "Beanie mania" had swept across the Atlantic, fuelled by announcements that certain toys in the range would be discontinued – thus pushing up the prices and the collectability. Then, in 1999, Ty made the bombshell announcement that all Beanie production would stop on December 31st 1999. Consequently, Beanie mania reached fever pitch and many a Beanie Baby is now well beyond pocket money range.

Frank

Frank is a faithful replica of a 1906 American bear from the collection of Dee Hockenberry, the well-known American teddy bear historian, writer, collector and erstwhile bear designer. The original Frank became famous when he appeared on a 32 cent stamp on February 3, 1998 as part of the "Celebrate the Century" commemorative stamp series, his name proving especially apt for the selection. This replica of Frank was designed by Dee Hockenberry and Frances Harper in an edition of two thousand and was launched in December 1999 on the eve of the millennium. It was nominated for a Golden Teddy award in 2000.

Dee was one of the American designers whom I met in 1993 when she showed her artist bears at the Northampton Convention and made me very aware of the changing face of collectors' teddy bears from across the Atlantic.

Millennium Bears

The year 2000 brought a crop of millennium-inspired bears ranging from Steiff bears to Beanie Babies. I particularly liked this pair of Dean's bears, Nightfall and Golden Dawn, in black and gold. They symbolise the passing century and dawn of the new millennium. I have shown them here celebrating that special New Year with a Harrods millennium bear.

My Little China Teddy

My Little China Teddy is the work of Amy Goodrich who launched her Portobello Bear Company in 1996. Amy studied sculpture at St Martin's School of Art in London, and as a student she loved to explore the antique markets. There she collected many of the old textiles and ephemera that were to prove the background and inspiration for the characters that she was later to make.

The inspiration for this little bear comes from the ritual of the English tea-table, with its mixed associations of cucumber sandwiches and historical links with China. As with all Amy's creations, one is very aware of a long gestation period in which an eclectic mix of ideas and hours of patient stitching eventually give birth to a bear that is very special.

When I first became aware of Amy's bears I found them particularly fascinating. They are very much artist bears, each one being an individual character, a real masterpiece of workmanship produced with huge creative flair, but the basic shape and inspiration also look back at a bygone age. It took Amy many hours to produce the cross stitched, sampler-like textile that she used to make this bear, and it is this blend of old and new that makes her Portobello bears so special. These are bears with one foot in the past and the other very much in the future. They look at me with the same captivating boot-button look to which I first succumbed. Yet they are bears that truly belong in the twenty-first century and will become heirlooms for the twenty-second and beyond.

Little Friend Bear

Little Friend Bear is from Steiff's Kleine Freunde toy range for babies. It is good to know that the smallest child can still enjoy the comfort of a well designed bear of classic heritage. Recently I have had the feeling that the teddy bear has been hijacked out of the nursery to become, predominantly, an expensive adult toy. The very young, on the other hand, are being fobbed off with cheap products of unattractive design that bear very little relationship to what one always thought of as a traditional teddy bear. Steiff, though, have not forgotten their founder's message, first proclaimed a hundred years ago, "Only the best is good enough for children".

Afterword

As we near the hundredth anniversary of that Mississipi bear hunt and Richard Steiff's first jointed toy bear, it would seem that the teddy bear has come a full circle. He has survived huge surges of popularity, deep troughs of decline, two World Wars and competition from cheap and alien merchandise, and yet has managed to retain a toe-hold in the nursery. His popularity, now, far exceeds that of the Bärenjahren of the early part of the century, and stretches well beyond the confines of the nursery. He has also become much more highly valued, both in monetary terms and as a desirable, collectable object.

Neither Richard Steiff nor Morris Michtom could have dreamt that their little toy bears would, a hundred years on, have come to mean so much more to so many people. Nor could they possibly have imagined the strange evolutionary forces that would change the shape and concept of their original creations, in some cases almost beyond recognition. But above all they probably never thought that their little toy bears would prove to be such powerful symbols of love and comfort to so many different people, young and old, the length and breadth of the globe.

Acknowledgements

I would like to thank the many people who have allowed me to draw their bears during the past twenty years and also all those who have helped, in anyway, with the compilation of this book.

Joanna Arkley
Arundel Toy and Military Museum
The late Anna Awdry
Irene Bacon
The Bear Museum, Petersfield
Tulip Bemrose
The Bethnal Green Museum of
 Childhood
Valerie Bishop
Rev. Michael Bishop
Roy Bishop
John and Margaret Burrows
Viv Challens
Marianne and Jürgen Cieslik
Pinky Daniel
Audrey Duck
Edinburgh Museum of Childhood
June Gardner
Marcelle Goffin
Amy Goodrich
The late Pam Hebbs
The late Colonel Bob Henderson
Brian Hick
Dee Hockenberry
Hove Museum and Art Gallery
Robert Ingpen
Jocelyne Jimenez
Laurence Koe
Naomi Laight
Arnelda Latimer
Colin and Wendy Lewis
The London Toy and Model
 Museum

Janice Longhi
Elaine Lonsdale
Hamish Maxwell-Stewart
Lucy Maxwell-Stewart
Neil Miller
Sue Pearson
Wendy Phillips
Pollocks Toy Museum
Ian Pout
Marie Robischon
The late Joan Robinson
James Roose-Evans
Carol-Lynn Rössel Waugh
The Royal Military Academy,
 Sandhurst
Pat Rush
Helga and Manfred Schepp
Ruth Snider
John and Judy Sparrow
Carol Ann Stanton
Margarete Steiff GmbH
Simon Theobalds
The Thurston Family
The late Marjorie Tutt
Paul and Rosemary Volpp
Brigid Waddams
Leon Warnholtv
Geraldine Wheeler
Sandra Wickenden
Sylvia Willgoss
Jack Wilson
Carrie Wiltshire

I would like to thank Pat Rush for reading the manuscript; Rosemary Lanning for editing it and for much useful advice; Nick Wells and Lucy Bradbury for the design and repro and Claire Dashwood of The Foundry for bringing it all together and, finally, a special thank you to my family for bearing up with it so gallantly over the years.

Permissions

Brian Hick – Teddy © 1986 *by kind permission of the author*
Simon Theobalds – King © 1988 *by kind permission of the author*
Sylvia Willgoss – My Old Teddy © 1999 *by kind permission of the author*

The design of the teddy bears shown in this book remain the copyright of each named bear artist or manufacturer.